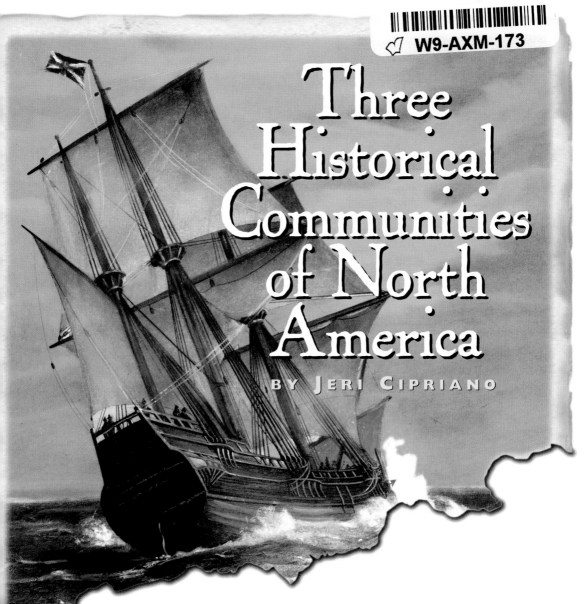

Three Historical Communities of North America

BY JERI CIPRIANO

Table of Contents

Introduction

Ready to take a trip across the United States of America long before it became a country? In this book, you will visit three historical communities, or groups of people, from the past.

The first stop is in the Southwest a thousand years ago. Meet Native Americans called the Anasazi (ah-nuh-SAH-zee). Learn about their **culture** (KUHL-cher), the way they lived. Then travel to the east coast in the 1600s. Find out about two other historical communities, the **colonies** (KAH-luh-neez) at Jamestown and Plymouth.

Mesa Verde was a Native American community in the Southwest. ▶

Why did these groups of people settle where they did? How were their communities alike? How were they different? What can we learn from how they lived? Step back in time and discover the answers.

◀ Jamestown was one of the first communities in the New World.

The Pilgrims ▶ started a community in Plymouth.

Chapter 1

Mesa Verde

More than a thousand years ago, Native Americans called Anasazi lived in an area of the Southwest called **Mesa Verde** (MAY-suh VER-dee). They shared the same **traditions** (trah-DIH-shuhnz), which are ways of living and doing things.

The Anasazi, whose name means "ancient ones," were the first known people in North America to build **permanent** (PER-mah-nehnt) homes that would last a long time. Their homes can still be seen today.

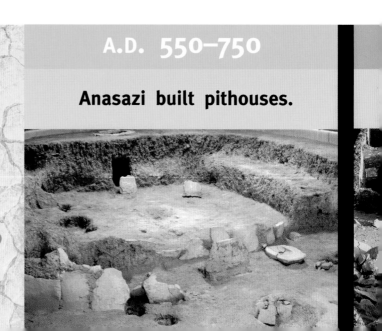

Anasazi Homes Through the Years

A.D. 550–750

Anasazi built pithouses.

It's a Fact

The Anasazi people lived in an area we call "the four corners." This is where the states of Colorado, Utah, Arizona, and New Mexico meet.

Over the years, Anasazi homes changed. First, Anasazi built pithouses into the ground. Then they built **pueblos** (PWEHB-lohz), which are groups of homes around an open space. Later, they built houses right into the cliffs.

Why did they build into cliffs? Maybe they wanted to keep cool during long, hot summer days. Maybe the high places would protect them from their enemies.

A.D. 750–1100

Anasazi built pueblos.

A.D. 1100–1200

Anasazi built homes in the side of cliffs.

Daily Life

The Anasazi lived on flat ground above steep rock walls. This high, flat land is called a **mesa** (MAY-suh). They grew corn, squash, and beans. They hunted small animals such as deer, sheep, and turkeys. They made stone tools. And they traded goods with each other.

The women spent a lot of time grinding corn and cooking. They also made beautiful pots, bowls, and plates with clay and sandstone. They painted the pottery black or red. Much of the pottery was used for cooking and storing things.

Black and white ▶ shapes decorate most Anasazi pottery.

They Made a Difference

On December 18, 1888, Richard Wetherill and his brother-in-law were the first to discover the Cliff Palace at Mesa Verde. Because of their work, we know more about this place and its people.

▼ We know more about the Anasazi people by studying Cliff Palace.

It's a Fact

Pueblo is a Spanish word that means "village." *Mesa Verde* means "green table" in Spanish.

Anasazi men spent a lot of time in their **kiva** (KEE-vuh). This was a kind of pit dug into the ground. They held important events there. They shared stories and celebrated their beliefs. Children and women were not welcome in the kiva. It was for men only.

Sometimes Anasazi men used a ladder to go dow

Then, around A.D. 1300, the people of Mesa Verde left the area. No one knows why. Maybe there was a drought (DROWT), a long period without rain, and they could not grow crops. Maybe the climate changed, and people couldn't grow food or find enough to eat.

Myth or Reality?

Did the Anasazi people just disappear? Some people think they went south and joined the Hopi (HOH-pee) and Zuñi (ZOON-yee) peoples of Arizona and New Mexico. Are we sure? No. What we do know is that they never returned to Mesa Verde.

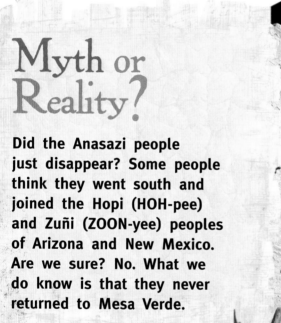

The Anasazi ▶ built stone ladders to get from place to place. Some dwellings reached as high as four stories.

9

Chapter 2
Jamestown

Virginia

The date is Sunday, April 26, 1607. Three ships from England reach the shores of the New World. They carry 104 men and boys. Rich men in England have paid for them to come to North America. They are settlers with dreams of starting a colony, a community that belongs to a country that is far away. They are going to look for gold and other goods to sell in England. They will also try to find a route to the Pacific Ocean.

The settlers decided to live on a long strip of land that stuck out into the water. They named the piece of land Jamestown, after their king. Today, this land is part of the state of Virginia.

The settlers worked all the time. They cut down trees. They built a fort and houses. But life was hard. The food they brought from England was running out. They fished and hunted some. But still, the settlers almost starved.

The hot, sticky weather added to the settlers' problems. They battled heat, bugs, and sickness. And Native Americans attacked them. That first summer, half the settlers died.

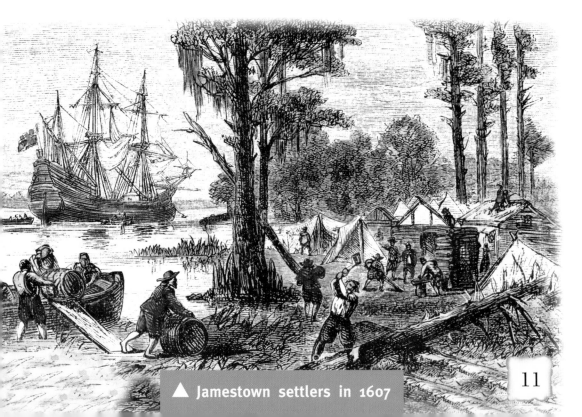

▲ Jamestown settlers in 1607

Then, in 1609, their first leader, John Smith, got hurt. He went back to England. In 1610, Lord De La Warr became the new leader. He brought 300 men and supplies. He brought food to end the starving.

By this time, some women had come to Jamestown. They helped the colony grow. They planted small gardens with carrots, beets, and other foods.

✔Point

Talk About It

Do you think the climates at Mesa Verde and Jamestown were the same? Share your thoughts with someone who is reading this book.

Jamestown Artifacts

Today, archaeologists (AHR-kee-ah-luh-jists) dig in the area of the Jamestown settlements. They are looking for things that the settlers used. They have found more than 150,000 items. Here are a few:

▼ hunting tools

The rich soil was good for planting. In 1612, settler John Rolfe began growing tobacco (tuh-BAH-koh). This crop was popular in England, but it didn't grow there. By 1619, Jamestown shipped ten tons of tobacco to Europe. By 1639, 750 tons were shipped! Growing tobacco made the colony rich.

The settlers' long, hard work paid off. Jamestown became the first permanent settlement in North America.

a silver ▶ coin from 1602

Jamestown settlers used blue glass beads to trade with Native Americans.
▼

13

Chapter 3

Plymouth

Massachusetts

Imagine it is September 1620. You and your parents board the *Mayflower* and set sail for North America. You reach what is now Plymouth (PLIH-muhth), Massachusetts (Mas-uh-CHOO-sehts). It is mid-December and very cold. You miss your home in England. But you will not go back. You are a **Pilgrim** (PIHL-grim) heading for a new life in a new land.

The Mayflower ▶ stayed away from shore for a month. The Pilgrims were looking for a good place to land. They pulled to shore on December 21, 1620.

Many Pilgrims went to North America because they wanted to follow their own religion. And they wanted to follow their own rules of government.

While still on the ship, the Pilgrims wrote the Mayflower Compact. This agreement set the rules for the colony. Each man had one vote. The colony's first leader, called a **governor** (GUH-vehn-er), was John Carver. But he died the following year. He was replaced by William Bradford.

▲ Pilgrims signed the Mayflower Compact.

Solve This

In 1621, William Bradford became the second governor of Plymouth. He was governor for thirty years. What was the last year Bradford was governor?

Math ☑ Point

Does your answer seem reasonable?

Daily Life

The settlers, who were also called **colonists** (KAH-luh-nihsts), built their own houses. They grew their own food. They made their clothes and other things such as candles and soap.

Many families were large. And every child worked! Girls helped cook, sew, or take care of small children. Boys fished and hunted. Both boys and girls took care of the farm animals. Children did not go to school. Their parents taught them to read.

◄ Pilgrim families cooked, worked, and slept in one room.

The rocky soil didn't allow people to have big farms like those in Jamestown. But they did grow corn and other crops. They also traded goods. They sent fur, fish, and wood to England. They made all kinds of goods that they traded among themselves.

Historical Perspective

When the Pilgrims came to this country, they were looking for freedom. They sailed on ships. The trip took weeks. Today, people from around the world still come to this country to find freedom. But they can fly on airplanes and make the trip in one day.

These first colonists all lived and worked near one another. They helped each other with different chores. And they attended church together.

The meeting house was important to the whole community. It was used as a church and as a place to talk over community business.

▲ Pilgrim meeting house

Good Friends

Unlike the Jamestown settlers, the Pilgrims got along well with the Native Americans. And the Native Americans helped them get through tough times.

They Made a Difference

Samoset and Squanto were two Native Americans who helped the Pilgrims. They showed the Pilgrims how to plant corn, tap maple trees, catch fish, and trap animals. They helped make a good harvest and the first Thanksgiving possible.

The Colony Grows

As time went on, Plymouth became successful, too. More colonists came to the New World. They spread out and settled in other places in North America.

Other communities began to form. Towns grew into cities. By 1733, there were thirteen colonies in all.

Not too long after that, the colonists fought for their freedom from England. A new, free country called the United States of America was born. And the first brave settlers had made it all possible.

▲ All of the thirteen colonies were along the east coast of the Atlantic Ocean.

Conclusion

You have just read about three different communities of the past. The Anasazi people were master builders. Jamestown settlers set up the first English colony in North America. And the Pilgrims at Plymouth were the first to settle in New England.

Today, you can visit the places they settled. You can see what life was like in these historical communities.

Use the pictures on page 22 to help you talk about the three communities. Talk about the people's homes, their hardships, and how they lived.

Point

Read More About It

Ask your teacher or librarian to help you find answers to these questions: How was the Jamestown community like the Plymouth community? How were the two communities different?

Visit Historical Communities Today

◀ These children at Mesa Verde National Park are learning first-hand what the cliff homes were like.

This fort at Jamestown has been rebuilt. It shows how life was in the early 1600s. ▶

◀ Workers at Plymouth **Plantation** (plan-TAY-shuhn) dress up in Pilgrim clothes.

Glossary

colony (KAH-luh-nee) a community that belongs to a country far away (page 2)

colonist (KAH-luh-nihst) a person who lives in a community that belongs to a country far away (page 16)

culture (KUHL-cher) the habits, traditions, and beliefs of a group of people (page 2)

governor (GUH-vehn-er) a person chosen to carry out the laws of the colony (page 15)

kiva (KEE-vuh) a Hopi word that means "ceremonial room"; a round dugout used as a meeting place (page 8)

mesa (MAY-suh) a landform that has a flat top and steep rock walls (page 6)

Mesa Verde (MAY-suh VER-dee) a national park in southwest Colorado where Anasazi ruins are preserved (page 4)

permanent (PER-mah-nehnt) lasting for a very long time or always (page 4)

plantation (plan-TAY-shuhn) an area in a hot place where crops are grown (page 22)

Pilgrim (PIHL-grim) an English person who settled at Plymouth, Massachusetts, hoping to worship there freely (page 14)

pueblo (PWEHB-loh) a Spanish word that means "village" which refers to a kind of Native American building in which small homes are joined together (page 5)

tradition (trah-DIH-shuhn) a custom or way of behaving that has continued for a long time in a group (page 4)

Index

Solve This
Answer

Page **15**

1621 + 30 = 1651

Math Checkpoint

Your answer is reasonable if it showed a higher number in the 1600s.